NUGGET AND DOG

ALL KETCHUP, NO MUSTARD!

written and illustrated by
JASON THARP

Ready-to-Read *GRAPHICS*

SIMON SPOTLIGHT

An imprint of Simon & Schuster Children's Publishing Division • New York • London • Toronto • Sydney • New Delhi
1230 Avenue of the Americas, New York, New York 10020 • This Simon Spotlight edition June 2021

To all the BIG dreamers,

Be yourself, stay kind, and try every day.
The right people will find you!
And to Beth, Laura, Siobhan, and Nicole,
K.E.T.C.H.U.P. Crusaders indeed!

—J. T.

Aunt Corny

Crouton
(say: KROO-tahn)

Dijon (say: dee-ZHON)
Mustard

Dog

Great-Grandpa
Frank Furter

Mayo Naze

Nugget

Tater Todd

Stomp

CONTENTS

How to Read This Book

This is Dog. He is here to give you some tips on how to read this book.

If there is a box like this one, read the words inside the box first. Then read the words in the speech or thought bubbles below it...

It's me, Dog! The pointy end of this **speech bubble** shows that I'm speaking.

When I'm thinking, you'll see a **bubbly cloud** with little clouds or circles pointing to me.

5

Chapter 1

FAST FORWARD TO NOW...

7

They are neighbors.

They are best friends.

They do everything together.

One day Great-Grandpa Frank Furter let them look for cool old stuff in his attic when...

Chapter 2

13

14

15

Chapter 3

Meanwhile, Nugget and Dog were opening the cool box.

That's it?!

A mask, a paper, and a photo?

One day we found out that someone named Mayo Naze was making evil plans.

Through the power of K.E.T.C.H.U.P., we began to ruin Mayo Naze's plans by being so kind to her that she forgot to be mean.

Another time Mayo Naze was sick, and we brought her a get-well card.

27

It didn't happen right away, but over time the mold went away, Mayo Naze changed her ways, and Gastropolis returned to normal.

By the way, I think you know her great-grandson, Dijon.

Chapter 4

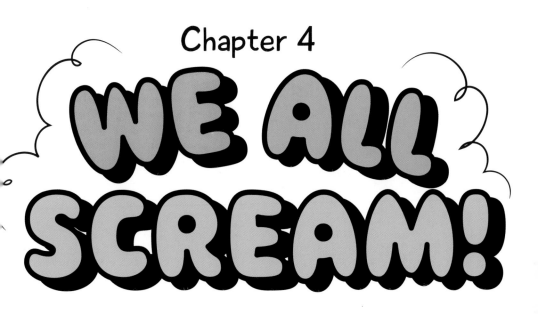

Later in the week...

Now is the perfect time to launch G.R.U.M.P.S.!

GIANT
REAL
UGLY
MONSTERS with
PERFECT
SCOWLS

G.R.U.M.P.S. is my greatest evil plan yet, and Stomp will be the first monster. Gastropolis will never know what hit it!

36

Chapter 5

Meanwhile, Nugget and Dog were spreading K.E.T.C.H.U.P. all around.

41

43

46

Chapter 6

Chapter 7

Everyone thinks 'cause I'm small I can't do anything. I can do big things too.

Tater Todd, you just used **empathy**, a K.E.T.C.H.U.P. power!

Do you want to be my friends? Boy, I wish I had some beans to share.

Chapter 8

56

What are you doing, Stomp?! You're supposed to be an evil monster.

But Stomp is not bad. **You** are bad. You lied to Stomp!

You are not a good guy.

Chapter 9